**Editor**
Eric Migliaccio

**Managing Editor**
Ina Massler Levin, M.A.

**Illustrator**
Vicki Frazier

**Cover Artist**
Barb Lorseyedi

**Art Manager**
Kevin Barnes

**Art Director**
CJae Froshay

**Imaging**
Rosa C. See
Craig Gunnell
James Edward Grace

**Publisher**
Mary D. Smith, M.S. Ed.

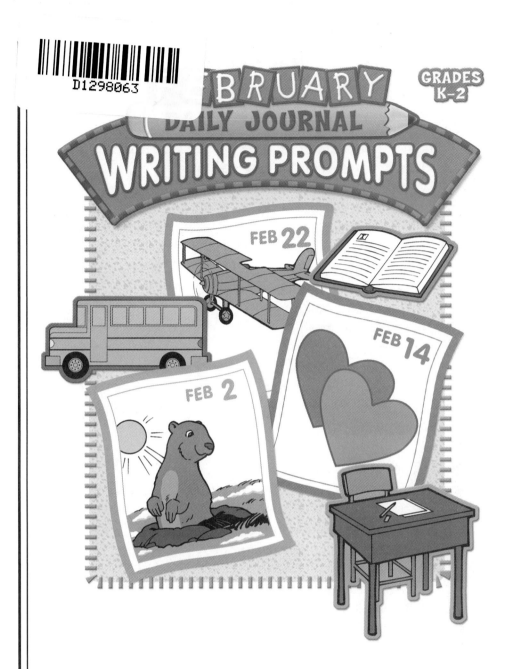

# FEBRUARY
## DAILY JOURNAL
# WRITING PROMPTS

GRADES K-2

FEB 22

FEB 14

FEB 2

**Author**

*Maria Elvira Gallardo, M.A.*

Teacher Created Resources

***Teacher Created Resources, Inc.***
6421 Industry Way
Westminster, CA 92683
www.teachercreated.com
**ISBN-1-4206-3131-4**
*©2005 Teacher Created Resources, Inc.*
Made in U.S.A.

# Table of Contents

# Introduction

More than ever, it is important for students to practice writing on a daily basis. Every classroom teacher knows that the key to getting students excited about writing is introducing interesting topics that are fun to write about. *February Daily Journal Writing Prompts* provides kindergarten through second grade teachers with an entire month of ready-to-use journal topics, including special holiday and seasonal topics for February. All journal topics are included in a calendar that can be easily reproduced for students. A student journal cover allows students to personalize their journal for the month.

Other useful pages that are fun include:

✣ **A Blank Calendar (pages 6 and 7)**

This can be used to meet your own classroom needs. You may want your students to come up with their own topics for the month, or it may come in handy for homework writing topics.

✣ **Word Banks (pages 40–43)**

These include commonly used vocabulary words for school, holiday, and seasonal topics. A blank word bank gives students a place to write other words they have learned throughout the month.

✣ **February Author Birthdays (page 44)**

Celebrate famous authors' birthdays or introduce an author who is new to your students. This page includes the authors' birthdays and titles of some of their most popular books.

✣ **February Historic Events (page 45)**

In the format of a time line, this page is a great reference tool for students. They will love seeing amazing events that happened in February.

✣ **February Discoveries and Inventions (page 46)**

Kindle students' curiosity about discoveries and inventions with this page. This is perfect to use for your science and social studies classes.

Motivate your students' writing by reproducing the pages in this book and making each student an individual journal. Use all the journal topics included, or pick and choose them as you please. See "Binding Ideas" on page 48 for ways to put it all together. Planning a month of writing will never be easier!

# Monthly Calendar

## F E B R

| | | | |
|---|---|---|---|
| **1**<br>The cutest animal I've ever seen is… | **2**<br>When the groundhog sees its shadow… | **3**<br>My favorite subject in school is… | **4**<br>If I could fly a plane… |
| **9**<br>I wish I could build… | **10**<br>If animals could talk… | **11**<br>When I get money… | **12**<br>Abraham Lincoln was… |
| **17**<br>I was mean to someone when… | **18**<br>This month I've learned… | **19**<br>My best friend and I always… | **20**<br>If there were no television… |
| **25**<br>If I lived underwater… | **26**<br>My family… | **27**<br>When I have a problem, I talk to… | **28**<br>I get grouchy when… |

# Monthly Calendar *(cont.)*

## UARY

| 5 | 6 | 7 | 8 |
|---|---|---|---|
| I want to learn how to speak… | I want to have a party for… | One day while playing at home… | An important African American is… |
| **13** | **14** | **15** | **16** |
| I have trouble learning how to… | Valentine's Day is fun because.. | My teacher helps me… | I get nervous at school when… |
| **21** | **22** | **23** | **24** |
| Swimming is fun because… | We celebrate George Washington's birthday because… | At school, I don't like to… | I wish I had a… |

| 29 | Special Topics |
|----|----------------|
| My favorite song is… | **Winter:** The best part of winter has been . . . <br> **Valentine's Day:** I want to make Valentine cards for . . . <br> **Presidents' Day:** The president is supposed to . . . |

# Blank Monthly Calendar

| F | E | B | R |
|---|---|---|---|
| 1 | 2 | 3 | 4 |
| 9 | 10 | 11 | 12 |
| 17 | 18 | 19 | 20 |
| 25 | 26 | 27 | 28 |

# Blank Monthly Calendar (cont.)

| U | A | R | Y |
|---|---|---|---|
| 5 | 6 | 7 | 8 |
| 13 | 14 | 15 | 16 |
| 21 | 22 | 23 | 24 |
| 29 | Free Choice Topics | | |

## The cutest animal I've ever seen is

_____

_____

_____

_____

_____

_____

_____

# When the groundhog sees its shadow

_____

_____

_____

_____

_____

_____

_____

_____

# My favorite subject in school is

_____

_____

_____

_____

_____

_____

10

# If I could fly a plane

# I want to learn how to speak

_____

_____

_____

_____

_____

Hola! Como esta?

_____

_____

_____

# I want to have a party for

_____

_____

_____

_____

_____

_____

# One day while playing at home

_____

_____

_____

_____

_____

_____

# An important African American is

_____

_____

_____

_____

_____

_____

_____

_____

# I wish I could build

# If animals could talk

_____

_____

_____

_____

_____

_____

_____

_____

# When I get money

# Abraham Lincoln was

_____

_____

_____

_____

_____

_____

_____

_____

# I have trouble learning how to

_____

_____

_____

_____

_____

10
12
6
+ 7
_____

_____

_____

# Valentine's Day is fun because

_____

_____

_____

_____

_____

_____

# My teacher helps me

_____

_____

_____

_____

_____

_____

_____

# I get nervous at school when

_____

_____

_____

_____

_____

# I was mean to someone when

_____

_____

_____

_____

_____

# This month I've learned

_____

_____

_____

_____

_____

_____

# My best friend and I always

_____

_____

_____

_____

_____

_____

26

# If there were no television

_____

_____

_____

_____

_____

_____

# Swimming is fun because

_____

_____

_____

_____

_____

_____

_____

# We celebrate George Washington's

birthday because _____

_____

_____

_____

_____

_____

_____

_____

# At school, I don't like to

_____

_____

_____

_____

_____

_____

# I wish I had a

# If I lived underwater

# My family

# When I have a problem, I talk to

_____

_____

_____

_____

_____

# I get grouchy when

_____

_____

_____

_____

_____

_____

_____

# My favorite song is

_____

_____

_____

_____

_____

_____

# The best part of winter has been

_____

_____

_____

_____

_____

_____

# I want to write Valentine cards for

_____

_____

_____

_____

_____

_____

# The President is supposed to

_____

_____

_____

_____

_____

_____

# School Word Bank

| | | | |
|---|---|---|---|
| alphabet | desks | map | recess |
| art | eraser | markers | report card |
| assembly | flag | math | rules |
| award | folder | note | science |
| binder | glue | office | scissors |
| board | grades | paper | spelling |
| books | history | pencils | study |
| bus | homework | pens | subject |
| children | journal | playground | teacher |
| clock | lessons | principal | test |
| crayons | lunch | reading | write |

# Holiday Word Bank

## February Holidays

| | |
|---|---|
| Groundhog Day | African-American History Month |
| Presidents' Day | Valentine's Day |

| | | |
|---|---|---|
| achievement | freedom | pink |
| ancestors | friend | president |
| arrow | heart | pride |
| birthday | heritage | red |
| brave | hero | ribbons |
| candy | hibernate | shadow |
| card | history | slavery |
| civil rights | hole | soil |
| cloudy | honest | spring |
| dirt | lace | United States |
| events | letter | Washington |
| first | Lincoln | winter |
| flowers | love | |

# Seasonal Word Bank

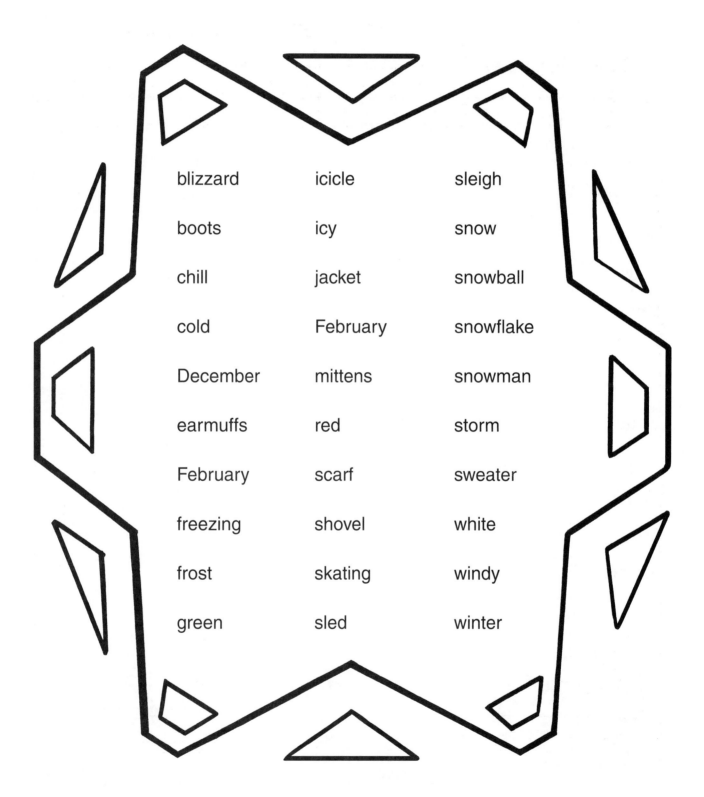

| blizzard | icicle | sleigh |
| --- | --- | --- |
| boots | icy | snow |
| chill | jacket | snowball |
| cold | February | snowflake |
| December | mittens | snowman |
| earmuffs | red | storm |
| February | scarf | sweater |
| freezing | shovel | white |
| frost | skating | windy |
| green | sled | winter |

# My Word Bank

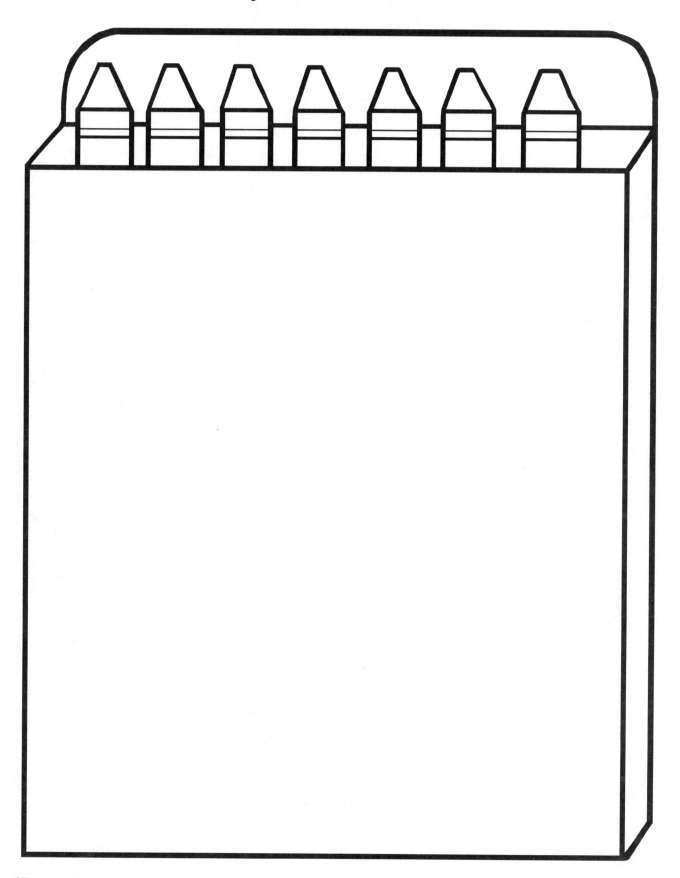

# February Author Birthdays

## 2

**Judith Viorst**
**(b. 1931)**

*Alexander And The Terrible, Horrible, No Good, Very Bad Day*
(Atheneum, 1972)
*Sunday Morning*
(Atheneum, 1992)

## 4

**Russell Hoban**
**(b. 1925)**

*A Birthday for Frances*
(HarperCollins, 1968)
*The Mole Family's Christmas*
(Scholastic, 1969)

## 5

**Patricia Lauber**
**(b. 1924)**

*Snakes Are Hunters*
(Harper Trophy, 1989)
*Be a Friend to Trees*
(Harper Trophy, 1994)

## 7

**Laura Ingalls Wilder**
**(1867–1957)**

*Little House on the Prairie*
(HarperCollins, 1953)
*Little House in the Big Woods*
(HarperCollins, 1953)

## 8

**Anne Rockwell**
**(b. 1934)**

*The First Snowfall*
(Simon & Schuster, 1987)
*My Pet Hamster*
(HarperCollins, 2002)

## 11

**Jane Yolen**
**(b. 1939)**

*Snow, Snow: Winter Poems*
(Boyds Mill Press, 1998)
*How do Dinosaurs Learn to Read?*
(Scholastic, 2003)

## 12

**Judy Blume**
**(b. 1938)**

*Freckle Juice*
(Yearling, 1978)
*The One in the Middle Is the Green Kangaroo*
(Yearling, 1982)

## 14

**George Shannon**
**(b. 1952)**

*Heart to Heart*
(Houghton Mifflin, 1995)
*Busy in the Garden*
(Greenwillow Books, 2005)

## 15

**Doris Orgel**
**(b. 1929)**

*A Dog's Tale*
(Gareth Stevens, 1996)
*The Bremen Town Musicians*
(Roaring Book Press, 2003)

## 19

**Louis Slobodkin**
**(1903–1975)**

*Wilbur the Warrior*
(Vanguard Press, 1987)
*Late Cukoo*
(Random House, 1988)

## 26

**Miriam Young**
**(1913–1989)**

*Miss Suzy*
(Mac Millan, 1964)
*So What If It's Raining!*
(Parents' Magazine Press, 1976)

## 27

**Laura E. Richards**
**(1850–1943)**

*Tirra Lirra: Rhymes Old and New*
(Little Brown & Co, 1955)
*Jiggle Joggle Jee!*
(Greenwillow Books, 2001)

# February Historic Events

**February 1, 1913**

New York City's Grand Central Station opened. It was the world's largest train station.

**February 4, 1789**

George Washington was elected to be the first President of the United States by the U.S. Electoral College.

**February 11, 1752**

Pennsylvania Hospital, the first hospital in the United States, opened.

**February 12, 1892**

Abraham Lincoln's birthday was declared a national holiday in the United States.

**February 12, 1909**

The National Association for the Advancement of Colored People (NAACP) was founded.

**February 14, 1849**

James Knox Polk became the first President of the United States to have his photograph taken.

**February 23, 1455**

This is traditionally considered the date of publication of the Gutenberg Bible, the first Western book printed from movable type.

**February 26, 1991**

Tim Berners-Lee introduced the first Web browser: WorldWideWeb.

**February 29, 1940**

Hattie McDaniel became the first African American to win an Academy Award, for her role in *Gone with the Wind.*

# February Discoveries and Inventions

**2** — **Buenos Aires, Argentina, was founded** in 1536 by Spaniard Pedro de Mendoza.

**3** — **First commercial cheese factory was founded** in Switzerland in 1815.

**6** — **Singapore was founded** by Sir Thomas Stamford Raffles in 1819.

**9** — **Volleyball was invented** in 1895 by William G. Morgan.

**10** — **YWCA was founded** in New York City in 1870.

**12** — **Santiago, Chile, was founded** by Pedro de Valdivia in 1541.

**18** — **Pluto was discovered** in 1930 by Clyde Tombaugh.

**The first "instant camera,"** the Polaroid Land Camera, was demonstrated in 1947 in New York City to a meeting of the Optical Society of America.

**21** — **Structure of the DNA molecule was discovered** in 1953 by Francis Crick and James D. Watson.

**23** — **Patent for the diesel engine was granted** to Rudolf Diesel in 1893.

**24** — **Patent for the steam shovel was granted** to William Otis in 1839.

**25** — **First U.S. electric printing press was patented** by Thomas Davenport in 1837.

# February Journal

by

_____

# Binding Ideas

Students will be so delighted when they see a month of their writing come together with one of the following binding ideas. You may choose to bind their journals at the beginning or end of the month, once they have already filled all of the journal topic pages. When ready to bind students' journals, have them color in their journal cover on page 47. It may be a good idea to reproduce the journal covers on hard stock paper in order to better protect the pages in the journal. Use the same hard stock paper for the back cover.

## Simple Book Binding

1. Put all pages in order and staple together along the left margin.

2. Cut book-binding tape to the exact length of the book.

3. Run the center line of tape along the left side of the book and fold to cover the front left margin and the back right margin. Your book is complete!

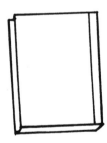

## Yarn-Sewn Binding

1. Put all pages in order and hole-punch the left margin.

2. Stitch the pages together with thick yarn or ribbon.

48